BALLET FOR BEGINNERS

Children's Ballet Class Photographs by Fred Lyon

Drawings by Margaret F. Atkinson

Music adapted and arranged by Beatrix B. Woolard

BALLET

FOR BEGINNERS

by Nancy Draper
and Margaret F. Atkinson

NEW YORK : ALFRED A. KNOPF

The authors and publisher wish to give credit as follows for the photographs used to illustrate this book:

Rothschild Photo, by Maxine Reams, Los Angeles: *Les Sylphides* [page 3]

Fred Lyon, from Rapho-Guillumette Pictures: Children's Ballet Class photographs [Jacket, frontispiece, pages 5–44]; Jocelyn Vollmar [pages 45–49]

Romaine, San Francisco: Jocelyn Vollmar [page 50]

Maurice Seymour: Ruthanna Boris and Leon Danielian [page 85]

Alfredo Valente: Janet Reed [page 86]

Serge Lido, Paris: and Moss Photo: Mary Ellen Moylan [page 87]

Bettmann Archive: *La Princesse de Navarre; La Liberazione di Tirreno* [page 88]

Harry Shaw Newman, The Old Print Shop, New York: Marie Camargo [page 89]; Marie Taglioni [page 90]

David Ashley, Inc.: *Pas de Quatre* (1845) [page 91]. From a color collotype reproduction of Chalon's *Pas de Quatre*, copyrighted 1945, by David Ashley, Inc.

Lincoln Kirstein: Vaslav Nijinsky [page 93]

Ballet Russe de Monte Carlo and Maurice Seymour: Alexandra Danilova [page 83]; Alicia Markova [page 94]; *Rodeo* (Nina Novak and Robert Lindgren) [page 98]

Original Ballet Russe: *Swan Lake* (Rosella Hightower and André Eglevsky) [page 95]

Larry Colwell: *Coppélia* (Danilova and cast) [page 96]; *Les Sylphides* (corps) [page 96]

Ballet Theatre and Maurice Seymour: *Bluebeard* [page 97]

Ballet Theatre: *Pas de Quatre* [page 91]; *Peter and the Wolf* [page 97]; *Fancy Free* [page 98]

Ballet Theatre and Rothschild Photo Los Angeles: *Giselle* (Alicia Markova and Anton Dolin [page 95]

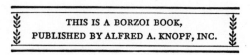

THIS IS A BORZOI BOOK,
PUBLISHED BY ALFRED A. KNOPF, INC.

Published February 19, 1951. Second printing, May 1951. Third printing, November 1951. Fourth printing, January 1952. Fifth printing, November 1952. Sixth printing, November 1954. Seventh printing, April 1958. Eighth printing, November 1964.

TO

THE PUPILS

WHO MADE

THIS BOOK POSSIBLE

Acknowledgment

The authors especially wish to express their gratitude to Muriel Stuart, staff member of the School of American Ballet, for the generous contribution of her time and for her help and encouragement in the preparation of this book.

The authors also wish to express their appreciation to Ruthanna Boris, Alexandra Danilova, Jocelyn Vollmar; to the many people in the Dance and Music Departments of the Museum of Modern Art, the New York and San Francisco Public Libraries and the Congressional Library; and to Betty A. Ferrell, Beatrix B. Woolard and May Hipshman for their valuable help in the preparation of this book.

Grateful acknowledgment is made to Alicia Markova, Janet Reed, and Mary Ellen Moylan for permission to use biographical material and photographs; to the children whose photographs illustrate the Ballet Class section and to their parents for permission to use these photographs.

Acknowledgment is also made to the following publishers for permission to use the musical works listed below as adapted and arranged for this volume by Beatrix B. Woolard:

The Boston Music Company for a selection from "Triumphal March" from *Peter and the Wolf* by Sergei Prokofieff, arranged by Chester Wallis; Editions Musicus for a selection from "Dance of the Ballerina" from *Petrouchka Suite* by Igor Stravinsky; Heugel & Cie for a selection from *Coppélia Ballet* (Scene #9) by Leo Delibes; W. Paxton & Co. Ltd., for selections from "Dance of the Swans" (Act II) and "Dance of the Swans" (Act IV) from *Swan Lake Ballet,* arranged for piano by Granville Bantock; G. Schirmer, Inc., for a selection from Chopin's *Nocturne,* Op. 32, No. 2, as edited, revised and fingered by Rafael Joseffy and a selection from the 3rd movement of the Chopin *Valse,* Op. 64, No. 2, revised and fingered by Raphael Joseffy.

CONTENTS

WHAT IS A BALLET?

Les Sylphides

Have you ever been bursting with joy and felt that you must tell someone about it?

All of us want to share our feelings and ideas with someone else. But everyone has a different way of doing it. A writer puts his ideas down on paper for you to read. A painter uses color to paint ideas for you to see. A musician puts his thoughts into musical sounds for you to hear. A dancer expresses ideas and feelings with movement for you to watch.

You will find that the first time you try to express your feelings by dancing your body doesn't do what you wanted it to do at all. That is because you have not yet taught and trained your body. Each artist has to learn and practice his own special art, in order to perfect it. It is only the trained artist who can make himself clearly understood.

A ballet is created by a group of artists working together. A ballet is a combination of the arts of movement, music, painting, and story.

A BALLERINA'S FIRST LESSON

Tamara Karsavina in Giselle

A full white tulle skirt — a fairylike figur
whirling across a dimly lit stage — beauti
ful music—applause. This is the dream o
almost every girl who studies ballet.

Tamara Karsavina, a little girl in Rus
sia sixty years ago, began to have suc
dreams. She begged her mother to tak
her to dancing school. Her mother knev
that the Imperial Ballet School in St
Petersburg would not teach children un
til they were eight years old. Tamar:
insisted, "But I am sure I can dance now!
Her mother, who also was sure her littl
girl could dance, arranged with a frien
who had been a famous dancer to giv
Tamara lessons until she was old enoug
to go to the Imperial Ballet School.

Tamara, hugging her first pair of balle
slippers, rang the doorbell at her teacl
er's house. She greeted her teacher, pu
on her slippers, and was ready to dance

Instead, she found herself holding on to a wooden rail that ran alon
the side of the wall, trying to get her feet into the strange positions th
teacher showed her. These, her teacher said, were the positions of th
feet which all ballet dancers must know. It was difficult for Tamara t
turn her toes out properly. In fact everything that she learned was diff
cult! She began to tire and wonder why she had to learn these strang
things when all she wanted to do was dance. The teacher told her to tur
around. Tamara, wanting to please her, tried to spin—and fell dowr
Her teacher laughed and said that she had only wanted her to tur
and face in the opposite direction. Tamara was embarrassed, hurt an
angry. When her teacher saw how really unhappy she was, she aske
her to sit down. Then she explained that all dancers must learn the balle
positions and exercises first, and that they must practice them over an
over again before they can spin and jump and dance.

"No girl can become a dancer just because she is talented and love
to dance," she said. "She must work very hard to become a dancer, an
even harder to become a ballerina."

Tamara Karsavina became a famous ballerina. She studied, sh
worked very hard, and she practiced, practiced, practiced.

Today pupils learn just the same ballet positions and exercises tha
Tamara Karsavina learned.

CHILDREN'S BALLET CLASS

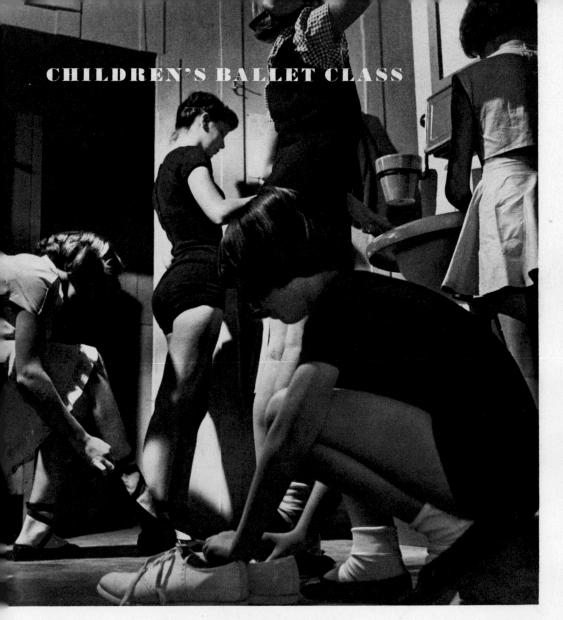

The Dressing Room

Pupils change into their practice clothes. Some pupils make their own practice clothes—often a short jumper or a brief circular skirt worn with a sweater or a blouse. The three girls in black snug-fitting costumes are wearing leotards.* This simple inexpensive cotton-knit costume is good for ballet class because the pupil as well as the teacher must be able to see the outline of the whole body in action.

The older girl ties the ribbons of her ballet shoes on the inside of her ankle near the back and tucks the ends securely under the ankle ribbon so they will look neat and not come unfastened when she is dancing.

Girls with long hair pin it up or tie it back in order to look sleek and keep their hair out of their eyes.

---

*Leotard (**Lee-o-tard**)   One-piece, snug-fitting cotton knit practice costume, originally designed by a French acrobat named Leotard.

"Shop Talk" about Slippers

These younger girls secure their slippers with an elastic band which is sewn across the instep of the slipper. They prefer the elastic band to ribbons which are difficult to tie.

The snug-fitting kid slippers are comfortable for beginners' feet. The slipper that is made with a pleated toe and a short sole (which extends just beyond the place where the toes join the foot) will not cramp the beginner's toes. This type of slipper allows the pupil to point her foot well, to strengthen her feet properly to prepare them for toe shoes.

The Rosin Box

Before ballet class begins, the pupils rub rosin* into the soles of their slippers as an extra safety measure against slipping.

---

*Rosin (**roz**-in)   As used here, tree sap in granular form having a sticky quality.

Professional on "Pointes," Beginner on "Half-Toe"

In soft leather ballet slippers the beginning pupil learns the ballet positions, exercises, and steps. She will have several years of training to strengthen and stretch her growing foot and leg muscles before she graduates to box-toed, reinforced satin toe shoes. This careful training prevents the development of knotty muscles and results in strong, shapely legs and feet.

Positions, exercises and steps learned in class on half-toe* are later done on *pointes*** by advanced students.

---

*Half-toe   On the ball of the foot—or *demi-pointe* (dem-ee **pwehnt**)
**Pointes   (pwehnt)   On the tips of the toes.

Eager Pupils Wait for Class to Begin

Before class begins some pupils practice at the *barre*.* Others laugh and chat while the pianist tries out music for the class. The first half hour of class instruction and practice is done at the *barre*. All *barre* exercises are designed to teach positions, to train the legs and feet to turn-out** and to strengthen and stretch all muscles. Some exercises are repeated as many as 32 times at the *barre* for each leg.

Barre (bar) A fixed wooden rail used by students to help keep balance while learning and practicing.
**Turn-out The turning out of the whole leg from the hip.

First Position

Heels together, toes opened out to the side.

Beginners face the *barre* to learn their positions because this makes it easier for them to stand correctly with their shoulders and hips straight and toes turned out. In order to turn the toes out the whole leg must be turned out and a child does this easily by tightening her buttocks muscles. Proper turn-out is essential for all positions and movements in ballet because it enables the dancer to move her legs and feet with greater freedom and ease.

It is quite permissible for the new pupil wearing socks to take this first class without slippers, but her dress makes it impossible for the teacher to see if she is learning to turn her legs out from the hips.

Second Position

First position opened by the length of one's own foot, with weight placed evenly on both feet.

Even though third position is not frequently used in ballet, all pupils must learn it. In third position the front foot is placed with heel touching instep of the back foot. Legs and feet must be well turned out.

These pupils are able to keep their shoulders straight and now need only one hand on the *barre*.

Older Pupils Stand in Third Position

Fourth Position

Heel of front foot is opposite toe of back foot. Feet are parallel and separated by the length of one's own foot. The weight is placed evenly on both feet.

Pupils learn that a correct position depends not only on the proper placing of the feet but also on the proper carriage of the whole body.

The first girl will be corrected for looking at the floor. The third little girl stands correctly in fourth position. Her feet are properly placed, legs turned out, back straight, shoulders down, head straight, and eyes front.

Corrections on Fourth Position

The Most Frequently Used Position — Fifth

These serious young pupils know that most steps begin and end with fifth position. In this position the feet are close together, with the front heel touching the toe of the back foot. Here as in all positions the legs and feet must be well turned out in order to do it correctly and the weight must be placed evenly on both feet.

Standing Straight Without Straining is Good Posture

This child was purposely chosen to demonstrate correct posture because she does not have a naturally straight back, but has the typical little girl's figure with rather plump buttocks. If she had not learned and practiced the rules for correct posture she would be sway-backed.

Five Basic Rules for Correct Posture

1. Place weight evenly on both feet.
2. Tighten stomach and buttocks muscles.
3. Raise diaphragm and ribs.
4. Push shoulders down.
5. Carry head high and straight.

These rules are repeated over and over again during class work. A pupil who has had several years of classic ballet training has good posture for the rest of her life.

Demi-Plié Stretches and Strengthens Young Muscles

*Demi-plié** is always the first exercise in the beginner's lessons. This slow half bend of the knees gently stretches and strengthens the leg muscles for a better turn-out position and prepares them for more strenuous exercises.

In *demi-plié* the weight must be correctly placed. The first girl will be reminded that she must not roll forward on her feet. The second girl is doing a correct *plié* — her feet are firmly on the floor and her weight centered on both feet.

Dancers *plié* before and after all jumps to avoid injury to their legs and knees. The *plié* gives a dancer greater elevation** and creates the appearance of ease and lightness.

Demi-plié (**dem**-ee-plee-ay) A half bend of the knees.
**Elevation The height to which a dancer can jump.

Beginners Try Demi-Plié in First Position

It is difficult for the beginner to remember to keep her buttocks muscles tight so that her seat is directly under her as she descends and opens her knees to the side.

Demi-Plié in Second Position

Demi-Plié *in Fourth Position*

Demi-Plié in *Fifth Position*

Students Advance to Grand Pliés

*Grand plié,** an exercise for more advanced pupils, is a continuation of *demi-plié*. Raising their heels and keeping them well forward and opening the knees out, the pupils descend in a *grand plié*. This stretches and strengthens the leg muscles for a good turn-out more completely than the *demi-plié*. All dancers "warm up" doing these *pliés* whether in class or before a performance.

Grand plié   (grahn plee-**ay**)   A full bend of the knees

Battement Tendu *to* The Front

Battement Tendu *to The Side*

Pupils Learn How to Move Their Feet

This exercise is called *battement tendu,** a small sliding kick in which the moving foot stretches to a full point and the toe remains on the floor. Both knees are kept straight. The pupils learn to keep their legs straight and move their feet with toes well pointed, arches lifted, and heels turned out.

---

*Battement tendu   (bat-**mah** tahn-**du**)   A small kick in which the tip of the toe slides and remains on the floor, with the knee straight and heel turned out.

This Exercise Makes Beautiful Insteps

Battement jeté* strengthens and stretches the instep and ankle. Similar to *battement tendu* with the knee straight and heel turned out, the toe leaves the floor in this small brush kick and is raised about 2 inches before returning to position.

*Battement jeté (bat-**mah** zhe-**tay**) A small brush kick front, side or back, in which the toe slides on the floor until the foot is fully extended and continues up off the floor about 2 inches.

Where To Place Foot and Leg for Turns

In a *pirouette*,* a turn on one foot, the raised foot and knee must be in position, not left dangling. The pupils learn to turn the knee out and place the raised foot *sur le cou-de-pied***—on the ankle of the other foot.

The *barre* exercise *sur le cou-de-pied* is a rapid changing of the foot in this position from front to back, with movement only from the knee.

---

*Pirouette (peer-oo-**et**) A turn or sequence of turns on one foot either on half-toe or on *pointe*.
***Sur le cou-de-pied* (**sur** le **coo** de **pyay**) One foot placed on the ankle of the other foot in a turned-out position.

Combinations of Two or More Exercises

The exercise *frappé** is a combination of *sur le cou-de-pied* and *battement jeté*.

In this exercise the foot is placed *sur le cou-de-pied* in front . . .

the underside of the toe just brushes the floor in a brisk kick to the side as the foot is raised and pointed . . .

*Frappé (fra-**pay**)   A small brush kick of the foot starting from and returning to the ankle.

the foot returns to *sur le cou-de-pied* in back . . .

the same motion is repeated returning foot to *sur le cou-de-pied* in front.

Younger Pupils Concentrate on Learning Ronds de Jambe

In *ronds de jambe à terre** the toe draws a semi-circle on the floor. This exercise is especially designed to train the leg and foot to turn out.

Ronds de jambe à terre **(rohn** de **zham** ba **tair)** A rapid semi-circular movement of the foot in which the toe remains on the floor and the heel brushes the floor in first position as it completes the semi-circle.

The pupil begins from first position . . .

foot slides front with toe well pointed and heel turned front . . .

toe slides to side . . .

toe slides to back . . .

foot returns to first position.

*Grand battement** is a large kick with knees kept straight. In this exercise it is easier for younger pupils to keep their shoulders down and hips straight when both hands are on the *barre*. The little girl in front has not yet learned to keep her shoulders down.

Grand battement strengthens the upper leg muscles and stretches legs for greater extension.****

For the Older Student Ronds de Jambe Becomes a Rapid Circular Motion

Learning Grand Battement at the Barr

Grand battement (grahn bat-**mah**) A high kick with straight knees to front, side or back.
****Extension The extending or raising of the leg as high as possible from the floor, knee straight.

**Grand Battement
To the Back**

This exercise not only stretches the legs but makes the back more supple for a beautiful *arabesque*.***

Learning Arabesque

***Arabesque** (ar-a-**besk**) A classic pose with the body supported on one leg, the other well extended to the back, the knees straight.

Good Turn-Out

*Passé** is the raised position of the leg before extending it. In this exercise, beginning from fifth position with the foot well arched, the toe is drawn up the inside of the leg with knee well turned out. *Passé* is also done rapidly to pass the leg from front to back.

Passé (pa-**say**) Passing the leg from front to back; or the raised position of the leg with foot at knee height before extending it.

Balance Comes with Strong Muscles

Strong back and stomach muscles as well as sturdy straight legs will help these young pupils balance in second position *relevé.** This is difficult and they cannot yet balance and keep their heels turned front.

Relevé (rel—**vay**) To rise up from the whole foot onto the ball of the foot, half-toe, or on to the *pointes*.

Échappé

*Échappé** beginning from fifth position *plié* is a quick slide of feet opening to . . .

second position *relevé*, pause, and return with a slide to fifth position *plié*. These girls should also have their heels turned front.

---

*Échappé (ay-sha-**pay**)* Staccato movement of the feet from fifth position *plié*, opening with a quick, springy slide to second or fourth position *relevé* and returning with a slide to fifth position *plié*.

The Whole Body Begins To Move

Pupils at the *barre* now learn to combine movement of the legs and feet with the arms and torso. *Port de bras** at the *barre* limbers the torso and makes the back supple.

Port de bras* (por** de **bra**)   A continual movement of the arms through a series of positions.

Stretching

Stretching with leg on *barre* develops greater extension. This is done in class only after muscles have become warm and pliant from other exercises.

Center Work

For the rest of the lesson pupils leave the *barre* and come to the center of the classroom to learn positions of arms, steps, jumps, turns. Some of the exercises learned at the *barre* are now repeated away from the *barre* to perfect turn-out and balance.

Gradually positions, steps, and movements are combined forming dance patterns—and the pupil begins to dance.

Positions of the Arms

Preparatory Position, often called fifth, is always the beginning position. Head and shoulders as well as arms and hands must be held correctly. If the right foot is in front, the torso is turned a little to bring the right shoulder forward and the head is turned slightly with eyes looking to the right. If the left foot is in front, the torso turns a little to the left. This carriage of the head and shoulders is called *épaulement*.*

*Épaulement (ay-pol-**mah**) Carriage and direction of the head and shoulders.

First Position of the Arms

Pupils raise their arms to first position. In learning positions of the arms it is important that the eyes and head follow movements of the hands because the head must not be held stiffly in one position.

Second Position

Arms and hands are opened out to the side to second position. When the right foot is front the eyes and head should follow the right arm and hand as it opens. There is only one girl who is doing this correctly.

Third Position

Arms are raised in third position. The continuous movement of the arms through these three positions will be a *port de bras*.

Pupils Use Mirror
To Study a Combination
of Arm Positions

One arm is raised to third position the other opened to the side to second. This pose is a combination of two arm positions. When the arm are in motion this becomes a *port de bras*. Arms always pass through fir position as they are raised and finis in preparatory position.

Movement of the Torso
With This Low Port de Bras

The pupil's head must follow the movement of her hands to make this *port de bras* beautiful. The girl at the back has spoiled the line of the movement by raising her head.

Learning First Arabesque

Arabesque requires good line, balance, and great extension. It is difficult for the beginner to balance, keep her back straight, her shoulders down, and make a long line from finger tip to finger tip while standing in a turned-out position with leg extended.

Four basic *arabesque* positions which vary with the positions of the arms and the direction of the body are learned in the classroom. On the stage a dancer may be given variations on the four basic *arabesque* positions.

Glissade

*Glissade** is a combination of two *barre* exercises, *demi-plié* and *batte-ment tendu* with a rapid transfer of weight from one foot to the other.

While learning simple steps and combinations pupils usually hold their arms in second position. Later they coordinate *port de bras* with the steps.

Glissade*   (glee-sahd**)   A connecting sliding step, usually done rapidly.

Glissade begins with *demi-plié* in fifth . . .

here quick *battement tendu* to second . . .

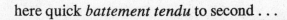

transfer weight immediately and . . .

quickly close to fifth in *demi-plié*.

Off the Floor

*Assemblé**: This jump needs quick thinking and good coordination. The little girl off the floor has found she can do it. The other two are trying. All jumps begin and end in *demi-plié*, heels on the floor. The little girl on the right is about to begin an *assemblé*. She will brush her right foot to the side, and at the same moment jump, landing in fifth position *demi-plié* with her right foot in front.

Assemblé* (ass-ahm-blay**) A jump in which one foot brushes off the floor at the moment of the jump and ends with both feet in fifth position.

This *jeté** when perfected becomes a dainty jump.

Jeté* (zhe-tay**) A small jump from one foot onto the other, beginning and ending with one foot raised *sur le cou-de-pied*.

Beginning in *demi-plié*, back foot raised, knee turned out . . .

foot brushes to side at moment of jump, knees straighten . . .

other foot is raised in back at finish in *demi-plié*.

Châinés turns* across the room are done by a series of steps with a half-turn of the body on each step. Steps are taken on half-toe and knees must be kept straight. For beginners arms are opened rapidly to second position and closed to first position with a whip-like movement—then a straight well-balanced body turns easily.

Châinés turns   (sheh-**nay** turns)   A sequence of spinning turns across the room, done by a series of steps on half-toe, legs straight, and a half-turn of the body on each step.

Ready . . .   Right foot steps out to second position
                                               on half-toe, arms open . . .

left foot steps to second position, the body makes a half-turn, arms close . . .

right foot steps to second position completing turn, arms open . . .
and continue sequence of turns.

Younger Pupils Try Turns

Younger pupils learn these turns slowly, stepping on the whole foot instead of half-toe.

Their backs are not yet strong, and they have difficulty keeping their balance.

A Trick for Turns

"Spotting" is a necessary trick. This means that you choose a place or spot in the direction you are going, keep your eyes on it as long as possible before turning your head, then quickly snap your head around to look at that spot again.

Spinning Across the Room — Châinés Turns

Trying for Greater Elevation

In this jump *changement de pieds*,* the position of the feet changes while in the air. The pupil begins from fifth position *demi-plié* with her right foot in front. She jumps and while in the air her front foot changes to the back and she lands in fifth position *demi-plié* with her left foot front.

Later, jumps are combined with a series of beats of the legs while in the air, and the famous *entrechat*** is learned.

Greater elevation allows a dancer to perform more beats in the air which makes a brilliant performance.

Changement de pieds* (shahzh-mah** de **pyay**) A small jump reversing the position of the feet while in the air. Beginning from fifth position the front foot goes to the back and the jump finishes in fifth.

Entrechat (ahn-tre-sha**) Similar to *changement de pieds*, this jump begins from fifth position, the legs beat front and back once or several times while in the air and the jump ends in fifth position.

A Seven-Year-Old Pupil Takes a Bow

Class is dismissed after this little bow. This formality is actually a curtain call for future ballerinas.

DAILY PRACTICE IS A PART OF
EVERY BALLERINA'S LIFE

Here young ballerina Jocelyn Vollmar, with the San Francisco Ballet Company, includes in her daily practice some of the same exercises that she learned as a child and that you have seen on the preceding pages.

Jocelyn Vollmar is wearing pink wool tights, a pink tunic and a black sweater. When a dancer's legs are kept warm, strenuous work is less tiring to the muscles. For this reason most dancers wear wool tights which they often knit themselves, using bright or pastel colors.

Grand Plié

Battement Tendu

Grand Battement

Arabesque

Port de Bras

Port de Bras

Stretching

Studying Line in the Mirror

Assemblé

Changement de Pied

Jocelyn Vollmar

This versatile and pretty young dancer has achieved the rank of ballerina. When Jocelyn was a little girl, before she went to ballet school, her mother taught her the positions of the feet and simple *port de bras* at home.

HOME PRACTICE

This is what you will need for your home ballet practice. First of all you must have a practice space. If the floors in your house are waxed and slippery use a thin rug with a pad under it to keep it from skidding, or a piece of linoleum.

Next, you must have a practice *barre*. This may be a table edge, the footboard of a bed, or the back of a chair, whichever is just the right height for you to rest your hands on comfortably, without reaching up or leaning down. Remember, this practice *barre* is to be used for balance only. Do not lean on it!

You should get soft leather ballet slippers.

Now you are all ready for your home ballet practice. You can practice at home the basic ballet positions that every ballerina has learned. But before you try these positions you must know the five rules for good posture. Here is a chart to help you learn them.

1. Stand the way you usually do but be sure to place your weight equally on both feet.

2. Tighten your stomach and buttocks muscles.

3.   Raise your diaphragm and ribs.   4.   Push your shoulders down.

5.   Carry your head straight and high.

Think of these posture rules every time you walk up or down stairs, every time you sit at the table to eat; say them out loud at least once a day; ask your friends to practice them with you.

BALLET PRACTICE FOR BEGINNERS

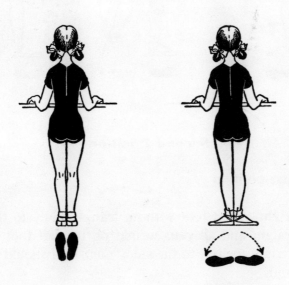

First Position

(1) Face practice *barre* and rest both hands on it lightly for balance. Put feet together and place weight evenly on both feet.

(2) Keep your heels together as you turn the toes of both feet out. Keep your knees straight! Your toes and heels should be in a straight line. You are now standing in the first ballet position!

While you are learning these positions of your feet, it is important to remind yourself that you must keep your weight a little more on the outer edges of your feet. If you find this too difficult, you may turn your toes slightly to the front until your feet and arches are stronger.

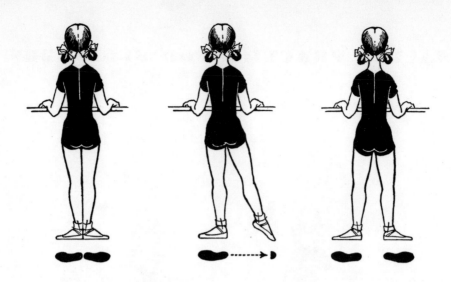

Second Position

(1)   From first position

(2)   Shift weight to left foot without leaning body to the left. Keep your knees straight and all your weight on the left foot as you point and slide your right toe out to the side. Your heel should be lifted and turned well front.

(3)   Place heel on floor and shift weight onto both feet. The space between your feet should be the length of one of your own feet. Now you are standing in second position!

To move your feet correctly from one position to another you must remember to:

> Raise your heel and turn it front as you point your toe.
> Keep your weight on the other foot as you point and slide your toe on the floor.
> Keep both knees straight.
> Keep your weight a little more on the outer edges of your feet in all of the ballet positions.

Third Position

(1)   From second position

(2)   Shift weight to left foot. Keep your knees straight and lift right heel turning it front while sliding right foot back toward left foot. Lower heel slowly as it approaches left foot.

(3)   Right heel passes left heel and is placed on floor, shifting weight to both feet. Feet are parallel with right heel in front of left arch. Now you are standing in third position!

Although third position is not frequently used in ballet, all ballerinas have learned it. You must learn it too. Next you will go to fifth position. Fourth position will come after fifth because it is easier to learn these positions in this way. Later, when you know your positions and when your feet are well trained, you can do them in their proper order.

Fifth Position

(1)   From third position

(2)   Keeping knees straight, slide right heel further in toward left toe. Try to make right heel touch left toe. Feet are together and weight equally distributed on both feet. Now you are standing in fifth position! This is the most frequently used position in ballet.

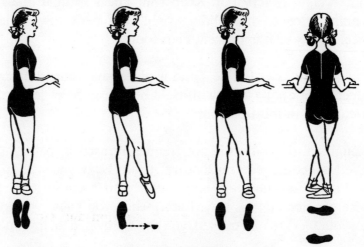

Fourth Position

(1)   From fifth position

(2)   Raise right heel and keep it turned front. Slide right toe to the front directly opposite left heel.

(3)   Put heel down, keeping it turned front, and shift weight to both feet. Feet are now separated by the length of one of your own feet. You are standing in fourth position!

You must keep your hips facing front, your knees straight, and weight on the outer edges of your feet. If you remember to tighten your buttocks muscles, it will be easier for you to keep your hips facing front.

Demi-Plié

Demi-plié is a half bend of the knees. This exercise gently stretches your leg muscles as you bend your knees and tightens them as you straighten. Dancers always begin their practice with *pliés*.

(1) Stand in first position facing practice *barre*.

(2) Keep your heels on the floor while you bend your knees slowly and open them out wide toward your toes. Keep your seat directly under you and your weight a little more on the outer edges of your feet.

(3) Come back up slowly to standing position and straighten your knees tightly.

Every time you do *demi-pliés* remember to:
> Keep your heels on the floor and your weight a little more on the outer edges of your feet.
> Open your knees out wide toward your toes.
> Keep your back straight and your seat directly under you.
> Move smoothly and continuously.

This is the way to practice *demi-pliés*. Count slowly:

You must move smoothly without stopping from the count of ONE right through to the count of FOUR.

While you practice ask someone to play this music from the ballet *Les Sylphides* by Chopin:

Nocturne [Op. 32, No. 2]

SIMPLIFIED

(Printed by permission of G. Schirmer, Inc., copyright owner.)

Lento   FRÉDÉRIC CHOPIN

Now try *demi-pliés* in these positions: first, second, fifth and fourth.

Battement Tendu

As you practice *battement tendu* your arches will become stronger and you will move your feet correctly with toes well pointed and heels turned front.

(1)   Stand in first position.

(2)   Keep your weight on your left foot, both knees straight, as you slide your right toe to point to second position.

(3)   Slide your right foot back to first position, heels touching, and keep your weight on your left foot so that the right foot is ready to repeat the exercise immediately.

When you practice *battement tendu* remember to:
>   Keep your weight entirely on the foot that is not moving.
>   Keep your knees straight.
>   Point and slide your toe on floor with heel raised and turned front.

Counting and Music for Battement Tendu

Count briskly:

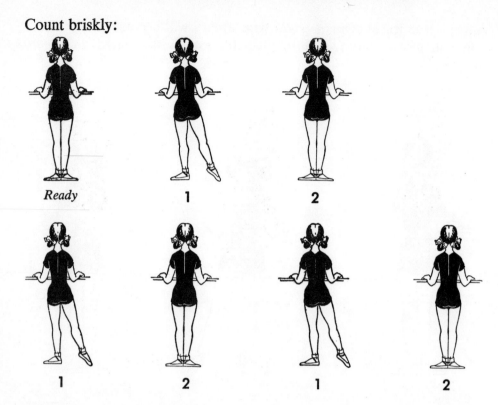

Ready   1   2

1   2   1   2

Use this brisk march from the ballet *Peter and the Wolf* for *battement tendu* practice:

Triumphal March [PETER AND THE WOLF]

(Printed by permission of The Boston Music Company, copyright owner.)

SERGEI PROKOFIEFF

Ready: 1 2 1 2 1 2 1 2 1 2 1 2 1 2 1 2

1 2 1 2 1 2 1 2 1 2 1 2 1 2 1 2

Combine Battement Tendu *with* Demi-Plié

Stand in first position before you begin.

(1)   Keep your weight on your left foot, with knees straight, as you slide your right toe to point to second position.

(2)   *Demi-plié* as you return your right foot to first position.

(3)   Repeat the exercise from the *demi-plié* position and as you slide your toe to point to second position straighten your knees.

Count:

Use this melody from the ballet *Swan Lake* when you practice *battement tendu* with *demi-plié:*

Dance of the Swans [from Act II]

SIMPLIFIED

(Printed by permission of the copyright owners, W. Paxton & Co. Ltd., London.)

Tempo di Valse   PËTR ILICH TSCHAIKOVSKY

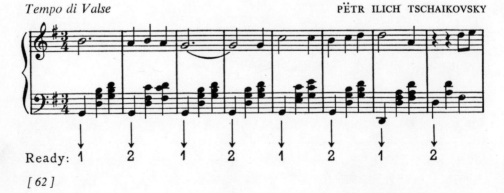

Demi-Plié *and Releve* in Second Position

Relevé means to rise up on the balls of the feet—half-toe. *Relevé* strengthens your feet and arches and also tightens and strengthens your leg muscles.
Stand in second position.

(1)   Begin with a *demi-plié*.

(2)   Keep your heels on the floor and straighten your knees. Then rise up onto half-toe keeping your heels front.

(3)   Lower heels to second position keeping knees straight.

For the *relevé* you must remember to:
    Keep your knees straight and your heels turned front on half-toe.

[63]

Count:

Ready   1   2   3   4

Use this lively music from the ballet *Pétrouchka* for *relevé:*

Dance of the Ballerina [PÉTROUCHKA]

(Printed by permission of Edition Musicus.)

IGOR STRAVINSKY

Positions of the Arms

Learn the positions of the arms away from your practice *barre*. In all positions, arms, hands, and fingers should be very slightly curved, never rigid, and you must always keep your shoulders down.

Preparatory Position

Stand in fifth position with your right foot front, turn your shoulders so that the right shoulder is a little more front.

Push your shoulders down and let your arms hang naturally. Bring your hands in front of your legs, curving your wrists a little so that your finger tips face each other. This is preparatory position. Your arms always start from and finish in this position.

First Position of the Arms

Your arms and hands are waist-high in front of you with almost no bend at the elbow. Finger tips almost touching and palms facing each other.

Second Position

Your arms are open to the side with almost no bend at the elbow and the palms of your hands face front.

Third Position

Arms are raised high, slightly forward of your head, with finger tips almost touching and the palms of your hands facing each other.

Other positions of the arms are combinations of these fundamental positions.

Port de Bras

Port de bras is a continual movement of the arms through a series of positions. To make your *port de bras* graceful move your arms smoothly and follow the movements of your hands with your head and eyes. Here are three simple *port de bras* for you to practice:

First Port de Bras

Preparatory position: Stand in fifth position with your right foot front. Turn your shoulders so that the right shoulder is a little more front.

(1)   Raise your arms to first position.

(2)   Open your arms to second position, eyes and head following your right hand.

(3)   Turn your hands so that your palms face down . . . raise your wrists slightly and lower them as you bring your hands down . . . to

(4)   Preparatory position.

Practice your *port de bras* to this count:

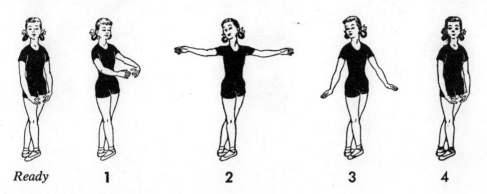

This delicate music from the ballet *Swan Lake* should help you move your arms gracefully:

Dance of the Swans [from Act IV]

SIMPLIFIED

(Printed by permission of the copyright owners, W. Paxton & Co. Ltd., London.)

Cantabile   PĒTR ILICH TSCHAIKOVSKY

Second Port de Bras

Preparatory position: Stand in fifth position with your right foot front. Turn your shoulders so that the right shoulder is a little more front.

(1) Raise your arms to first position.

(2) Raise your arms high to third position, eyes and head following the movements of your hands.

(3) Bring your arms down opening them out to second position.

(4) Turn your hands so that your palms face down . . . raise your wrists slightly . . . lower them bringing your hands down to preparatory position.

This music from the ballet *Les Sylphides* should inspire you to move your arms beautifully:

Valse [Op. 64, No. 2]

SIMPLIFIED

(Printed by permission of G. Schirmer, Inc., copyright owner.)

Combine First and Second Port de Bras

By combining these *port de bras* you will get the feeling of continuous arm movements through a longer series of positions.

Preparatory position: Stand in fifth position with your right foot front. Turn your shoulders so that right shoulder is a little more front.

(1)   Raise your arms to first position.

(2)   Open to second position.

(3) Turn your hands so that your palms face down, raise your wrists slightly, lower them

(4) To preparatory position.

(5) Without pausing raise your arms to first position.

(6) Now high to third.

(7) Open to second.

(8) Preparatory position.

Ready   1   2   3   4

5   6   7   8

When you practice these *port de bras* remember to:

Keep your shoulders down.

Make rounded lines with your arms, hands and fingers by keeping them slightly curved and moving them smoothly.

Always begin and finish in preparatory position.

Be sure your shoulders are in the correct direction. When you stand with your right foot in front, bring the right shoulder front, or with your left foot in front, bring the left shoulder front.

Use this lovely music from the ballet *Coppélia* for your combination of *port de bras:*

Coppélia Ballet [from Scene #9]

SIMPLIFIED

Andante con moto

LEO DELIBES

PRACTICE CHART
FOR BEGINNERS AT HOME

Practice the Five Positions at the Barre

Use your right foot to go from one position to the next:

FIRST POSITION

SECOND POSITION

THIRD POSITION

FIFTH POSITION

FOURTH POSITION

Now repeat, using your left foot to go from one position to the next:

FIRST POSITION

SECOND POSITION

THIRD POSITION

FIFTH POSITION

FOURTH POSITION

Practice these Exercises at the Barre

4 *DEMI-PLIÉS* in each of these positions, using your right foot to go from one position to the next:

FIRST POSITION—4 *DEMI-PLIÉS*

SECOND POSITION—4 *DEMI-PLIÉS*

FIFTH POSITION—4 *DEMI-PLIÉS*

FOURTH POSITION—4 *DEMI-PLIÉS*

Repeat, using your left foot to go from one position to the next:

FIRST POSITION—4 *DEMI-PLIÉS*

SECOND POSITION—4 *DEMI-PLIÉS*

FIFTH POSITION—4 *DEMI-PLIÉS*

FOURTH POSITION—4 *DEMI-PLIÉS*

16 *BATTEMENT TENDU* in first position, using your right foot.

16 *BATTEMENT TENDU* in first position, using your left foot.

16 *BATTEMENT TENDU* WITH *DEMI-PLIÉ* in first position, using your right foot.

16 *BATTEMENT TENDU* WITH *DEMI-PLIÉ* in first position, using your left foot.

16 *RELEVÉ* WITH *DEMI-PLIÉ* in second position.

At the finish take your hands off the *barre* and try to balance on half-toe (on the balls of your feet) in second position with your arms in second position.

Practice Port de Bras *Away from the* Barre

4 FIRST *PORT DE BRAS*, standing in fifth position, right foot front and right shoulder front.

4 SECOND *PORT DE BRAS*, standing in fifth position, left foot front and left shoulder front.

4 COMBINED *PORT DE BRAS*, standing in fifth position, right foot front and right shoulder front.

4 COMBINED *PORT DE BRAS*, standing in fifth position, left foot front and left shoulder front.

When you know the positions of the feet thoroughly, start your practice at the *barre* with the *demi-pliés*. After the *port de bras* you may repeat your *barre*-work (when you can do it well) without the aid of the *barre*.

GOOD POSTURE

You can pick out a dancer in a group of people by noticing the way she holds herself. Beautifully erect, she carries her head as though she were wearing a crown! All dancers have good posture. When they were little girls, not all of them had naturally straight backs. They learned good posture, just as they learned the positions of the feet.

You can look like a dancer if you learn these five simple posture rules and make them a habit by thinking of them all the time.

1. Stand as you would naturally and place your weight equally on both feet.

2. Tighten your stomach and buttocks muscles.

3. Lift your diaphragm and ribs.

4. Push down with your shoulders.

5. Carry your head high and straight.

Here is a good way to test yourself for correct posture:

Stand with feet together, your back to the wall, heels and head touching it. Using the five posture rules try to flatten your shoulders and whole back against the wall. You may not be able to do this the first few times you try, but after your muscles are trained you will have good posture from then on and this test will be easy for you.

When you have good posture your clothes will fit better and look better on you. You can actually make your waist smaller by tightening your stomach muscles and lifting up your ribs.

Push your shoulders down and hold your head high to have a pretty neck and shoulders.

You will have a firm figure if your muscles are trained by correct posture. You will not have the backaches and fatigue often caused by incorrect posture.

Your body is well balanced when your posture is correct. All sports will be easier for you to do well.

Good posture makes you look well and gives you a feeling of assurance.

BEHIND THE SCENES

A tremendous amount of work goes into the creation of a ballet. The ballet which you see is the result of the combined talents and efforts of a variety of artists. These are the artists who create a ballet:

The Choreographer

The choreographer arranges the dance patterns for a ballet. He selects the steps and movements and fits them to music for the dancers. These movements are planned to tell a story or to express a mood.

For the ballet *Swan Lake* the choreographer selected a fairy tale about a girl who was transformed into a swan. He arranged movements that made the dancers resemble swans.

The Composer

The composer writes the music to which a ballet is danced, and arranges it for an orchestra.

The melodious music for *Swan Lake* perfectly suggests the movements of swans.

The Designers of the Settings and the Costumes

The scenery is designed in color by an artist who plans the setting and lighting effects to suit the story or the mood of a ballet.

The setting for *Swan Lake* is a clearing in a forest by the side of a lake. The pale soft colors and dimly lit stage which the artist designed for this woodland scene make a perfect background for the swans.

The costumes are designed in colors by an artist to harmonize with the scenery and to fit the story.

In *Swan Lake* the full white tulle skirts, tutus, and white feather headdresses give the dancers the appearance of swans.

[80]

The Ballet Master or Mistress

The ballet master or mistress teaches and rehearses the dancers in their parts for a ballet. The dancers were taught and rehearsed for many hours before they were ready to dance *Swan Lake* for an audience.

The Dancers

All the dancers in a ballet company have been trained in the classical style of ballet, which is the learning of traditional ballet positions, steps, and movements.

The Corps de Ballet

The least perfected dancers, usually the younger members of a ballet company, who dance together as a group are the *Corps de Ballet*.

The Soloists

The soloists are the more accomplished dancers in a ballet company, who have worked hard to perfect their dancing. They are often graduates of the *Corps de Ballet*. Soloists dance small solo parts in a ballet as well as difficult variations requiring a group of two, three, or four dancers.

The Ballerinas and the Premier Danseurs

The ballerinas and the *premier danseurs* are the most accomplished dancers, who have earned their place as "stars" of a ballet company. They dance the most difficult and beautiful leading roles in a ballet.

The Prima Ballerina

This title, meaning "first ballerina," is not frequently used. It is earned by a dancer who has been well known as a ballerina for years and who, because of her experience and the flawless perfection of her dancing, is acclaimed by the public as one of the greatest dancers of her time.

The Musicians

The conductor and his musicians learn the scores written for a ballet. After many rehearsals with the dancers, the music and the dancing blend in perfect unison.

A ballet is produced with the work and help of many other people behind the scenes. These are *the persons back stage:*

The Stage Manager is the boss of all the workmen back stage as well as the dancers. He is completely responsible for the operation of each performance. He may have been trained as a dancer or a musician and therefore can properly cue the light and curtain men.

The Propertyman is in charge of the scenery and the props, and oversees the stage hands who change the scenery.

The Electrician, cued by the Stage Manager, manages the lighting effects for each scene, and oversees the men at the "spots" and "light-board."

The Carpenter is in charge of all the carpentry work for the sets.

The Flyman oversees the raising and lowering of the huge backdrops for the settings.

The Curtainman has the job of raising and lowering the curtain at precisely the right moments on the cue from the Stage Manager.

The Wardrobe Master and Mistress have charge of all the costumes. They see that the costumes are ready for each performance, help the dancers make quick changes between scenes, and are always on hand for last-minute touches during the tense moments just before the curtain goes up.

The Company Manager. As boss of the whole ballet company, from *prima ballerina* to carpenter, the Company Manager is held responsible for the operation of the ballet until the Stage Manager takes over just before each performance. He handles all the business affairs of the company. He checks each performance for flaws or possible improvements, and settles disputes among the temperamental artists.

BALLERINAS

Alexandra Danilova,
Prima Ballerina

"Dancing is not just moving, it is thinking!"

Although she studied every day when she was eight-and-a-half years old at the Imperial Ballet School in St. Petersburg, Alexandra Danilova was not very much interested in what she was learning. In her charming Russian accent she recalls that "During that first year I found it very difficult to concentrate and was told that I would be expelled from the School if I continued in this way. They gave me one more year to improve, so I made myself concentrate immediately!"

During her second year, Alexandra was given a walk-on part as one of the crowd in a performance of the opera *Faust* at the Marinsky Theatre. She was nervous and kept bumping into people in her eagerness to get to the front of the stage so that her parents would be sure to see her.

After many years of study, she became a ballerina.

She danced all over the world with famous ballet companies. Kings and queens presented her with beautiful jewels in token of their appreciation of her dancing. Now a *prima ballerina* with the Ballet Russe de Monte Carlo, her dressing room is constantly filled with flowers from her admiring public.

Hard work and concentration went into the many years that developed the eager child who bumped into people during her first performance into the world-famous *prima ballerina*, Alexandra Danilova.

Alicia Markova,
Prima Ballerina

"Your little girl is much too thin and delicate, Mrs. Marks, perhaps ballet lessons would build her up," advised the doctor. So eight-year-old English Alice Marks took ballet lessons, and her mother had great hopes that her daughter would become another Anna Pavlova. By the time she was nine years old she was strong and showed real talent, and her mother took her to a famous Russian ballet teacher, Madame Astafieva, who was then teaching in London.

Alice studied every day, and in a very few years she had made extraordinary progress. When she was perfect technically, she was the first English dancer to be invited to become a member of a Russian ballet company. With this company she dressed her shining black hair in the Russian style and changed her English name to the Russian-sounding name, Alicia Markova.

Alicia Markova is acclaimed as one of the greatest *prima ballerinas,* and has danced with many famous ballet companies including her own company.

She has been compared with the great Anna Pavlova because of her superbly delicate dancing and her fragile appearance. Strangely enough, Markova shows a resemblance to Pavlova in some photographs.

The doctor who prescribed ballet lessons to strengthen little Alice Marks certainly could never have dreamed that his small patient would one day become the famous *prima ballerina,* Alicia Markova!

Ruthanna Boris

From the time she was a very little girl, Ruthanna Boris was determined to be a ballerina. When she was ten years old she went to the Metropolitan Opera Ballet School in New York City and took classes three times a week during her first and second years. In her third year she took classes every day. For many years she worked very hard and studied at several different schools.

One day Ruthanna was stunned when a teacher impatiently said to her, "You'll never be a ballerina!" In tears she went to Muriel Stuart, a friend and teacher at the School of American Ballet, to ask her if this could possibly be true. Miss Stuart told her, "Darling, if you want to be a ballerina you can!"

Ruthanna wanted to so much and worked so hard that she became a ballerina and she has also become a choreographer.

Janet Reed

In the little town of Medford, Oregon, Janet Reed took ballet lessons twice a week. For several years, Janet wanted to dance in musical comedies until she saw a "one-night stand" of a visiting ballet company. From then on she wanted to be a ballerina. She realized that she must work harder, and, being a clever girl, she was able to do some secretarial work at the dancing school in exchange for daily classes. With her talent and hard work she became an outstanding dancer with the San Francisco Opera Ballet Company; later earned her rank as a ballerina and became a member of the New York City Ballet Company.

Petite, energetic, ballerina Janet Reed also finds time to do an excellent job of raising her son and to be a gracious hostess and homemaker for her husband.

Mary Ellen Moylan

Little Mary Ellen Moylan was practicing in her own "special" practice place in the big living room of their house in St. Petersburg, Florida, while her mother played the piano. All the neighborhood children pressed their noses against the window to watch. The middle of the floor was cleared and the space was never waxed because it was used only for practice. In addition to her two lessons a week, Mary Ellen practiced constantly at home. Her mother helped her and encouraged her because she recognized her daughter's talent.

For more intensive training Mary Ellen went to New York to study. At sixteen she danced with the New York Opera Company, and later she danced as a soloist with the Ballet Russe de Monte Carlo.

She soon became one of the youngest dancers with the rank of ballerina in the Ballet Russe de Monte Carlo.

HOW BALLET BEGAN

If you are invited to a ballet, you can picture what you are going to see at the theater—colorful stage settings; beautiful costumes; ladies dancing and whirling on the points of their toes; and men leaping and turning in the air.

If you had lived in Italy four hundred years ago, you might have been invited to a performance of a ballet at a nobleman's palace. You would have been surprised to see that there were no women dancing! Only men were allowed to dance in the ballets. They wore boots, tight-fitting trousers, doublets, large plumed headdresses, and masks covering their faces. The men danced slowly and sedately in rows to simple music played on reeds and pipes. The friend who had invited you to the palace might have been Catherine de Médicis, the young daughter of an Italian nobleman. This little girl, Catherine, later became engaged to Henri, a French prince. When she was still a very young girl, she married him and went to live at the French court in Paris.

When Catherine was older and became queen of France, she was a very powerful and commanding woman. She missed the ballet that she had loved in her own country, and ordered the dancers to come from Italy to dance at her court in Paris. Just because of the whim of this woman ballets were brought to France. For the next two hundred years the French were the greatest ballet dancers and ballet teachers in the world.

The ballets in Catherine's court in France would seem tiresome to us because there was little variety in the dance steps, and often one of the dancers stopped dancing to act out the story.

La Princesse de Navarre
at Versailles; after Cochin

La Liberazione di Tirreno
Florence, 1616. From etching by Callot

Marie Camargo

Long after Catherine died, the rich and great King Louis XIV, whose word was law, insisted on dancing the leading roles in some of the ballets. When Louis became too fat and old to dance he established the Royal Academy of Dancing and Music, the first school of dancing in France. Louis allowed women to study dancing at the Academy so that they too could dance in the ballets at his court. These Royal Academy dancers also performed in public theaters, where for the first time people who were never invited to the palace could see the ballets.

Since French customs, language, and arts were greatly admired in other countries, French ballet masters were invited everywhere to teach dancing. These Frenchmen taught in their own language, no matter what country they were in, and French became (and still is) the language for ballet. The steps that were taught in those days would seem easy to us for they were much simpler than they are now, and the movements were prim because the ladies were heavily corseted and could not move easily in their bulky floor-length dresses.

Unfortunately for Louis, who loved the ballet, he died before he was able to see one of the first great French ballerinas, Marie Camargo, dance in her daring new costume. This ballerina, who first danced in 1721, had the boldness to cut the skirt of her dress a few inches shorter so that she could dance more swiftly and show off her beautiful ankles. It is said that this startling lady also removed the heels from her shoes in order to dance with more liveliness. Later other dancers copied the length of her dresses and wore heelless slippers. In these shorter dresses and heelless slippers the dancers could learn new steps, jumps and turns, and it is believed that they then began to use two of the basic ballet positions that we learn now —first and fifth.

When Camargo grew older, perhaps she dreamed that a day might come when ballerinas would dance on the points of their toes. That day did come, but many years too late for Camargo. She would have been about one hundred years old when Marie Taglioni, the first great ballerina to dance with perfection on the points of her toes, was born in Sweden in 1804.

Marie Taglioni's father, a famous Italian dancer, took Marie to Paris when she was a little girl to study ballet at the great French Academy. Marie's father was very strict and made her perfect everything she learned until she was able to dance beautifully on the points of her toes. A graceful, long, white bell-shaped tulle skirt, called the *tutu*, was especially designed for Taglioni's dainty figure. Choreographers created ballets just for her—fantasies about flowers dancing in the meadows, or sylphs dancing in the glades. She jumped so high and was able to balance so perfectly on the points of her toes that she really appeared to be a fairy floating through the air.

Men have never learned to dance on their toes because their special role in ballet is to show great strength in contrast to the ladies' delicate dancing. The men are trained to make extraordinary leaps and many turns and to lift the ladies high in the air and support them in their difficult balanced poses.

The fantasy ballets created in Taglioni's time are called "Romantic" or "White" ballets. Long white *tutus* were worn in these ballets and the

Marie Taglioni
as the Fairy of the Flowers

Pas de Quatre (1845)
*Carlotta Grisi, Marie Taglioni,
Lucille Grahn, Fanny Cerito*

dancing was dainty and the posing exaggerated. Some of the first Romantic Ballets that were created for Taglioni would seem amusing to us, for often the dancers were suspended on wires and pulleys to make their flying entrances onto the stage. A few of the Romantic Ballets that were created later are still great favorites today. One of these, the famous *Pas de Quatre*, was created for Taglioni and three other ballerinas in Queen Victoria's time. The Queen commanded the four most famous ballerinas of her day, Marie Taglioni, Fanny Cerito, Carlotta Grisi and Lucille Grahn, to dance for her in London. These competitive ballerinas did not dare refuse the royal command. They danced just one performance together before the Queen—the *Pas de Quatre*, or dance for four—and then the jealous beauties refused ever to appear together again.

Pas de Quatre
*Nora Kaye, Alicia Markova,
Annabelle Lyon, Karon Conrad*

In Victorian days, beautiful dancers were trained in America and Europe, many of them taught by French ballet masters. Some of these dancers formed groups and travelled as ballet companies. There was even a group of children travelling as a ballet company at this time. They were trained in Austria and were called the Viennese Children's Ballet.

Now that ballet had become so popular, almost every opera that was written included a ballet. A law was actually passed in France saying that no opera could be given without a ballet. Some of Wagner's operas had to be rearranged to include a ballet before they could be performed in Paris.

Ballet audiences went wild over an especially beautiful performance. They stood and cheered and threw flowers onto the stage. Sometimes after a performance they would carry a ballerina on their shoulders through the streets. These people were true balletomanes. There is a story about Taglioni, when she danced in Russia, that some of her admirers bought her toe shoes for a huge price, stewed them in a large pot and then solemnly drank the broth! Whether this is true or not, the Russians were so inspired by Taglioni that the French ballet teachers at the Russian schools trained their own dancers to dance Taglioni's roles.

A group of touring Italian dancers came to Russia and astonished the Russians. They jumped higher and did more beats and turns than the Russian audience had ever seen before. The Russian dancers were tremendously impressed, but because they could not do these difficult things themselves, they claimed their own delicate French style of dancing was more beautiful. They spoke of the Italians as mere acrobats. Later, however, when the Italian ballerina Virginia Zucchi, danced in Russia and performed her amazingly difficult steps and wore a *tutu* cut off to the knee, the Russian dancers changed their minds about the Italian style of dancing. They then invited the great Italian dancer, Enrico Cecchetti, to teach them the difficult and brilliant Italian style of dancing, and they cut off their own *tutus* even shorter than Zucchi's.

When the Russians had learned how to do the dozens of *pirouettes* and the extraordinary leaps of the Italian technique, they combined these stunts with their delicate French poses and dainty steps. This combination of French and Italian techniques became Classic Ballet. The Russians made a special *tutu* for this new style of dancing—the classic *tutu*. This *tutu* was very short so that the dancers' legs were free to execute the vigorous turns and leaps for the Classic Ballets which often told stories about princes and princesses.

The two famous Russian Imperial Schools of Ballet, one at St. Petersburg, the other at Moscow, were crowded with young hopefuls in spite of the very strict entrance examinations at each school. These two schools were boarding schools and the pupils who were chosen had to devote their entire school years to dancing. The children received all their ballet training and school lessons free for these schools were supported by the Tzars. The applicants had to be ten years old and had to pass an examination to be allowed to study at the schools. The director and the head ballet masters chose the pupils carefully for appearance, health, natural grace, and feeling for music and rhythm. They were given a year's trial at the school. In order to remain there, the strictly-taught pupils had to show real progress in their dancing, lessons in art and music and dramatics, and in all their other studies.

The finest dancers in the world graduated from these Russian Ballet Schools between the time of Taglioni's death and the Russian revolution. One of their most brilliant stars was Anna Pavlova. People all over the world still speak of her with reverence. This fragile beauty seemed to cast a spell of enchantment when she danced in her perfect and delicate way. But she herself was never satisfied for even after she had reached the rank of *Prima Ballerina* she asked the great Italian maestro Enrico Cecchetti to give her private lessons.

The greatest male dancer in history was Vaslav Nijinsky, also from the Imperial School and one of Pavlova's partners. His dancing was magnificent and his leaps so spectacular that the audience was spellbound. When Nijinsky was asked how one could perform such leaps, he replied, "It is quite easy—you have merely to pause a little in the air and then come down again."

Vaslav Nijinsky

Alicia Markova

Pavlova and Nijinsky and the other great dancers of their time danced the famous Classic Ballets. Gradually these dancers and choreographers began to change the style of ballets because they found the movements and stories in the Classic Ballets so much alike that they could not express all of their ideas and feelings. Sometimes they wanted to dance a mood rather than a story—they wanted to dance with more freedom and use their arms in many more ways than the few positions used in the Classic Ballets—they wanted to dance barefoot or in sandals wearing many kinds of costumes as well as in toe shoes and *tutus*. The ballets that these dancers and choreographers created are called Modern Ballets.

Ever since the Russian revolution in 1917, excellent dancers have been trained in ballet schools all over the world. Some of these may even surpass the greatest dancers in ballet history—but unfortunately there is no way to compare them. How wonderful it would be if Marie Camargo, Marie Taglioni, Anna Pavlova and Alicia Markova were to compete for us in the *Pas de Quatre*.

Today you may find, all on the same program, one of the old Romantic Ballets, one of the famous Classic Ballets and also a Modern Ballet. The dancers are trained in the classic style because it is considered to be the most perfect method for training the body for ballet.

In the Modern Ballets of today that tell a story, the costumes and settings are sometimes of the present day—cowboys at a ranch, sailors on shore leave—or if the ballet is about people of old-fashioned days, the costumes are of that time. In Modern Ballets that express only a mood or a feeling, the costumes and settings are usually fanciful and are designed especially for line and color. In some of these ballets the dancers use straight movements of their arms and bodies rather than the rounded classic ones, just as some modern painters paint pictures in straight, angular lines rather than in curved and more realistic lines.

In these four hundred years many countries and countless dancers and artists have changed and influenced the style of ballet until it has become what you see today on the stage.

ROMANTIC, CLASSIC. AND MODERN BALLETS

Giselle, a Romantic Ballet

Swan Lake, a Classic Ballet

Coppélia, a Classic Ballet

Les Sylphides, a Modern Ballet in the Romantic Manner

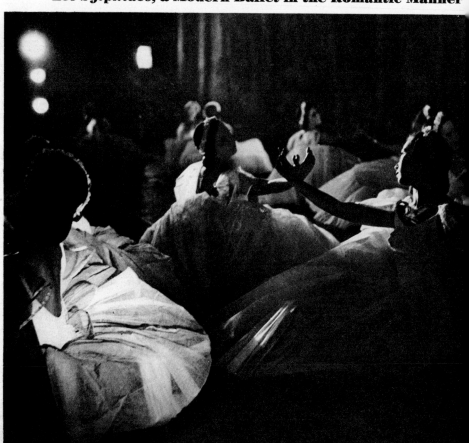

Bluebeard, a Modern Ballet [97]

Peter and the Wolf, a Modern Ballet

Rodeo, a Modern Ballet

Fancy Free, a Modern Bal

STORIES OF BALLETS
Especially Appealing to Young People

Giselle (zhee-**zehl**):   A Romantic Ballet in two acts in a fairy-tale setting.

In the first act, a peasant girl, Giselle, is in love with a prince who poses as a peasant. When the girl discovers that he is a prince and engaged to marry a princess, she loses her mind and dies of grief.

In the second act the prince visits her grave at night. The spirits in the graveyard come out and dance. Giselle's spirit steps out of her grave and dances with the prince. When she returns to the grave the prince is overcome with grief.

Pas de Quatre   (**pa** de **katr**):   A Romantic Ballet in one act.

In 1845, Taglioni, Cerito, Grisi, and Grahn, the four top-ranking and competitive ballerinas, were invited by royal command to give a special performance for Queen Victoria. The ballet was *Pas de Quatre,* a dance for four. The success of this ballet was enormous but the four ballerinas refused ever to appear together again.

The *Pas de Quatre* today is a revival of the original ballet and is performed by ranking ballerinas in the fashion of Queen Victoria's day with exaggerated politeness and the particular mannerisms of the four original ballerinas.

Swan Lake: A Classic Ballet originally in four acts, now usually done in two acts, set by the side of a lake in a forest.

This ballet is the story of a beautiful maiden, Odette, who has been transformed by a sorcerer into a swan. Each midnight, for one brief hour, the maiden resumes her human form. As the ballet opens, the swan glides across the enchanted lake in a forest clearing. A prince and his friends come to the lake to hunt. Just at midnight the swan appears as Odette, the Swan Queen, and begs the prince and his friends not to shoot her swans. The prince falls in love with Odette, and they dance together in the moonlight. But once again Odette falls under the sorcerer's spell and is transformed back into a swan, leaving the prince brokenhearted.

The Nutcracker: A Classic Ballet in two acts in a Victorian setting with fairy-tale scenes.

The ballet opens with a family Christmas party for a little girl and boy, Clara and Fritzi. Each guest brings a present, and the one Clara likes best is a nutcracker in the shape of a doll. When the party is over and the family has gone to bed, Clara dreams that the nutcracker doll comes to life and takes her to fairyland with him.

The next scene is a dream in which Clara and the nutcracker go to the Snow Country where the Snow Queen and the snowflakes dance.

In the second act, the dream changes to the Kingdom of Candy, where a celebration is given in Clara's honor on the terrace of the Palace of Sweets. She is entertained by the Sugar Plum Fairy and a variety of dancers.

Coppélia   (ko-**pehl**-ya):   A Classic Ballet in two acts in a provincial village setting.

The first act is set in an old kingdom of Spain. Swanhilda, who is in love with Frantz, becomes jealous of a mysterious figure at the window of a strange old man's house. Swanhilda and her friends manage to enter the house.

In the second act they find that this mysterious figure is a life-sized mechanical doll, Coppélia. Swanhilda changes clothes with the doll when she hears the old man returning to his house. The old man wishes to show Frantz, who has climbed in through the window to see what is going on, his magic powers over this doll. Swanhilda falls in with this plan and pretends to be his doll coming to life. When the old man discovers he has been tricked he is very unhappy, but Frantz and Swanhilda, who are about to be married, make amends by giving him a bag of gold.

Les Sylphides   (lay sill-**feed**):   A Modern Ballet in the costume and mood of a Romantic Ballet, in one act in a forest-glade setting.

This ballet does not tell a story. It expresses a fairylike mood in which woodsprites dance in the moonlight in a forest glade.

Pétrouchka   (pay-**troosh**-ka):   A Modern Ballet in three acts, set in old Russia.

This ballet tells the story of three puppets, a clown named Pétrouchka, a dancer, and a blackamoor. The first act shows a Russian street carnival, where a crowd of people enjoy themselves watching the side-shows. A magician appears. One by one he brings his three puppets to life to perform for the crowd.

In the second act, Pétrouchka and the blackamoor are in the cells where the magician keeps them between performances. The dancer visits each of them and Pétrouchka and the blackamoor get into an argument over her.

In the third act, when the puppets are performing again, the blackamoor gets out of the magician's control and strikes the clown with his sword. The crowd watches horrified, believing that a man has been murdered. However, when the magician reminds them that after all Pétrouchka and the blackamoor and the dancer are only puppets, the crowd leaves. The magician, left alone, is dragging the puppet clown away when he is stopped by a cry. It is Pétrouchka's spirit calling out from the roof top!

La Boutique Fantasque   (la boo-**teek** fahn-**task**):   A Modern Ballet in one act set in a toyshop.

Customers come to a French toyshop and order toys from the shopkeeper. Late that night the toys leave their boxes and play pranks on each other. The following morning the customers return to the shop and complain that the toys have not been delivered. The shopkeeper reassures them, but on opening the boxes he finds that the toys have disappeared! At that moment the toys come back and gleefully chase the angry customers away. The shopkeeper is so overjoyed to have them back that he decides never to sell them.

Le Beau Danube   (le **boh** da-**nube**):   A Modern Ballet in one act set in old Vienna.

Tumblers and a group of strolling actors put on a show in a park. A young girl and her fiancé, a handsome Viennese officer, stroll by and watch the performance. A street dancer who has been in love with the officer appears and jealously starts a fight with the young girl, which causes a great commotion. The dancer tries to entice the officer by dancing with him; however, in the end he pleads with his fiancée to forgive him, which she finally does.

Gaîté Parisienne   (geh-**tay** pa-reez-**yen**):   A Modern Ballet in one act in an old-fashioned setting.

Gay people arrive at a Parisian outdoor restaurant in the time of Napoleon and amuse themselves by dancing. A pretty young glove-seller falls in love with a baron, and a funny little Peruvian rug-seller tries to take her away from him. An argument develops and all the men get into a fight. The rug-seller is finally chased away and everybody dances cheerfully until late at night when the restaurant closes.

Graduation Ball: A Modern Ballet in one act set in old Vienna.

The pupils of a fashionable Viennese girls' boarding school have invited boys from a near-by military academy to their graduation dance. The elderly headmistress of the school and the headmaster of the boys' school have a flirtation. This amuses the young people, and the party is a very gay affair.

Bluebeard: A Modern Ballet originally in four acts in a medieval setting.

The story in this ballet is adapted from the fairy tale *Bluebeard*. Bluebeard has killed five of his wives by poisoning them. He plots the murder of his sixth wife, Boulette, in order to marry a seventh. Boulette, however, outwits him. Finally, after many complications, the King allows Bluebeard to divorce Boulette, who is delighted to be rid of him, and Bluebeard is free to marry again.

Peter and the Wolf: A Modern Ballet in one act in a present-day setting.

Despite warnings about the wolf, Peter and his friends, the duck, the bird, and the cat, go into the forest. There they meet the wolf who seizes the duck and runs off with her. Peter finally lassoes the wolf and ties him to a tree. While he is wondering what to do with him, some huntsmen arrive, and they all decide that the zoo is the place for the wolf. Then they march away happily to the zoo with the wolf in tow.

Rodeo: A Modern Ballet in two scenes in a present-day setting.

In the first scene, cowboys hold contest in a rodeo at Burnt Ranch. A cowgirl competes with the men while the rancher's daughter and her friends watch her with disapproval.

In the second scene everyone is gathered in the ranch house for a dance. The cowgirl, still in her jeans, is a wallflower, but when she changes into a dress, she outshines the rancher's daughter and her friends.

Fancy Free: A Modern Ballet in one act in a present-day setting.

Three sailors on shore leave amuse themselves in a small New York café. Two girls arrive and the three sailors get into an argument over them. When the sailors begin to fight, the girls are frightened and leave. After the girls have left, the sailors patch up their quarrel and decide that they have been very foolish to fight over girls. As the sailors leave the café another girl walks past and all three dash off in pursuit of her.

adagio (a-**dah**-jo): A slow movement in a ballet often danced by a ballerina and her partner.

arabesque (ar-a-**besk**): A classic ballet pose. The body is supported on one leg, the other well extended to the back with knee straight. Positions of the arms and torso vary.

assemblé (ass-ahm-**blay**): A jump with one foot brushing off the floor at the moment of the jump, both feet coming together in fifth position at the finish.

ballerina (bal-e-**ree**-na): A female "star" in a ballet company. Ballerinas dance the leading rôles in a ballet.

   Prima Ballerina (**pree**-ma bal-e-**ree**-na): Highest ranking ballerina in a company.

ballet (**bal**-ay or ba-**lay**): A ballet is a story, part of a story, an idea, or a feeling, expressed in dancing to the accompaniment of an orchestra.

balletomane (ba-**let**-o-main): A person who loves the art of ballet, a frequent ballet-goer and enthusiast about everything concerning ballet.

ballet shoe: A soft leather slipper worn while learning and practicing ballet. Also worn during performances by male dancers and sometimes by female dancers when their parts do not require the use of toe shoes.

barre (bar): A fixed wood rail used by dancers to help keep balance while learning and practicing.

battement jeté (bat-**mah** zhe-**tay**): A small brush kick, front, side, or back, in which the toe slides on the floor until the foot is fully extended and continues up off the floor about two inches.

battement tendu (bat-**mah** tahn-**du**): A small kick in which the tip of the toe slides and remains on the floor, with the knee straight and heel turned out.

chaînés (sheh-**nay**): A sequence of spinning turns across a room or stage done by a series of steps on half-toe or on *pointes* with both knees straight and a half turn of the body on each step.

changement de pied (shahzh-**mah** de **pyay**): A small jump reversing the positions of the feet while in the air. Beginning from fifth position, the front foot goes to the back and the jump finishes in fifth.

choreographer (ko-ri-**og**-ra-fer): A person who selects the steps and movements and arranges them in dance patterns to fit the music for a ballet.

choreography (ko-ri-**og**-ra-fi): The composition of steps, movements, and dance patterns in a ballet.

corps de ballet (**kor** de ba-**lay**): The dancers in a ballet who dance together only as a group.

décor (day-**kor**): The French term for stage settings.

demi-plié (**dem**-ee plee-**ay**): A half-bend of the knees, in any of the five positions, keeping heels on the floor and knees opened out toward the toes.

divertissement (dee-vair-tees-**mah**) or variation: Usually a brilliant and difficult sequence of steps in a ballet danced by a ballerina, a *premier danseur,* or a soloist.

échappé (ay-sha-**pay**): A staccato movement of feet from fifth position *plié,* opening with a quick, springy slide to second or fourth position *relevé,* and returning to fifth.

elevation: The height to which a dancer can jump.

entrechat (ahn-tre-**sha**): Similar to *changement de pied,* this jump begins from fifth position, the legs beat front and back once, or many more times while in the air, and the jump ends in fifth.

épaulement (ay-pol-**mah**): Carriage and direction of the head and shoulders.

extension: The extending or raising of the leg with straight knee as high as possible from the floor.

fouetté (foo-ay-**tay**): A series of turns on one leg, the other leg extending rapidly to the side and whipping the body around.

frappé (fra-**pay**): A small brush kick of the foot starting from and returning to the ankle.

glissade (glee-**sahd**): A connecting sliding-step, usually done to the side.

grand battement (grahn bat-**mah**): A high kick with straight knees to the front, side, or back.

grand jeté (**grahn** zhe-**tay**): A leap from one foot onto the other, usually done from a running start or from a glissade.

grand plié (**grahn** plee-**ay**): A full bend of the knees, in any of the five positions, with heels raised and knees opened out wide toward the toes.

half-toe or demi-pointe (**dem**-ee pwehnt): On the ball of the foot.

jeté (zhe-**tay**): A small jump from one foot onto the other, beginning and ending with one foot raised *sur le cou-de-pied.*

leotard (**lee**-o-tard): A one-piece, snug-fitting cotton knit practice costume.

pas (pa): A combination of steps forming one dance.

pas de bourrée (**pa** de boo-**ray**): Tiny fluttering steps on *pointes* done by shifting weight rapidly from one toe to the other.

pas de deux (**pa** de **der**): A dance for two performed by the ballerina and her partner; often the romantic part of a ballet.

pas de quatre (**pa** de **katr**): A dance for four.

pas de trois (**pa** de **trwa**): A dance for three.

passé (pa-**say**): Passing the leg from front to back, or the raised position of the leg with foot at knee height before extending it.

pirouette (peer-oo-**et**): A turn or sequence of turns on one foot, either on half-toe or on *pointe*.

pointes (pwehnt *or* pwan't): On the points of the toes.
    Demi-pointe (**dem**-ee pwehnt *or* **dem**-ee pwan't): Half-toe.

port de bras (**por** de **bra**): A continual movement of the arms through a series of positions.

premier danseur (**prem**-yay dah-**ser**): A male "star" who dances the leading rôles in a ballet and partners the ballerina.

relevé (rel-**vay**): To rise up from the whole foot onto half-toe, *demi-pointe,* or *pointes.*

ronds de jambe à terre (**rohn** de **zham** ba **tair**): A rapid semicircular movement of the foot in which the toe remains on the floor and the heel brushes the floor in first position as it completes the semicircle.

rosin (**roz**-in): Granulated tree sap rubbed into soles of slippers or on points of toe shoes to prevent slipping.

soloists: The dancers in a ballet company, often graduates of the *corps de ballet,* who dance small solo parts or in groups of two, three, or four.

sur le cou-de-pied (**sur** le **coo** de **pyay**): One arched foot placed on the ankle of the other foot in a turned-out position.

turn-out: The turning out of the legs from the hips. The turned-out position enables the dancer to move legs and feet with greater ease.

tutu (**tu-tu**): Romantic *tutu*—a long, many-layered, bell-shaped skirt of tarleton, worn in "Romantic" or "White Ballets."
    Classic *tutu*—A very short, many-layered tarleton skirt, worn in "Classic Ballets."

CATHERINE DE MÉDICIS (1519–1589). Italian wife of Henri II of France. Introduced Italian ballet to the Court of France in 1581.

LULLY, JEAN BAPTISTE (1632–1687). French musician, composer, and dancer, born in Italy. Under Louis XIV he helped create the Académie Royale de Musique et de Danse of which he became director in 1672.

LOUIS XIV (1638–1715). King of France, patron of the arts and balletomane. Often danced in court ballets himself. Sponsored the establishment of an Academy of Dancing which became the Académie Royale de Musique et de Danse in Paris, and now is the Théâtre National de l'Opéra.

BEAUCHAMP, PIERRE (1639–1705). French dancer. Became ballet master in 1671 at the Académie Royale in Paris. Dancing master to King Louis XIV. Brilliant dancer who helped lay foundation of ballet techniques.

PRÉVOST, FRANÇOISE (1680–1741). French dancer and teacher at the Académie Royale, and *première danseuse* at the Paris Opéra. Trained Camargo and Sallé.

SALLÉ, MARIE (1707–1756). French ballerina, rival of Camargo. Trained at the Académie Royale in Paris. She was not a virtuoso like Camargo, but was famous for her naturalness and expressiveness. Like Isadora Duncan, she sometimes danced in a tunic with her hair loose and flowing.

CAMARGO, MARIE (1710–1770). French ballerina of Spanish descent. Trained at the Académie Royale in Paris. One of the first tremendously popular ballerinas, she introduced the shorter skirt and is credited with introducing the heelless slipper. She excelled in swift and brilliant use of feet and leg movements, and it is said that she was the first woman to perfect the *entrechat*.

NOVERRE, JEAN GEORGES (1727–1810). French choreographer and reformer of old-style ballet. Did away with traditional wearing of masks and changed the stiff conventional movements of the dancers. Wrote more than a hundred and fifty ballets. His famous notes on dance and ballet were published in 1760.

VESTRIS, GAÉTAN (1729–1808). French dancer and teacher of Italian descent. Studied at Académie Royale in Paris and became soloist and *maître de ballet* in 1761. One of Louis XIV's dancing masters, he was an outstanding dancer of his day. Chiefly noted as the father and first teacher of his famous son, Auguste Vestris.

HEINEL, ANNA (1753–1808). German ballerina. Trained at Stuttgart Theatre. A great virtuoso, she is credited with being the first to perform the multiple *pirouette*.

VESTRIS, AUGUSTE (1760–1842). French *premier danseur* and teacher. Trained by his father, he was the greatest male dancer of his time. He was *premier danseur* at the Paris Opéra for 36 years, and was known for his arrogance as well as his brilliance. Among his pupils at the school of the Opéra were Charles Didelot and Jules Perrot.

DIDELOT, CHARLES (1767–1837). French dancer, choreographer, and teacher. Studied in Sweden with his father, later with Vestris in Paris. Choreographer at the Imperial Ballet in St. Petersburg. His Romantic Ballets were the first to have interesting plots, and he made use of mechanical devices for flying entrances onto the stage. He originated the now traditional flesh-colored tights for women.

TAGLIONI, FILIPPO (1777–1871). Italian *premier danseur* and choreographer. Father of Maria Taglioni. Ballet master and *premier danseur*, Stockholm. His most famous ballet, created for his remarkable daughter, was *La Sylphide*.

CORALLI, JEAN (1779–1854). French dancer and choreographer. Trained at the Opéra Ballet School, Paris. After successfully staging ballets in Milan and Marseilles, he became choreographer of the Paris Opéra, where he did ballets in the Romantic style.

BLASIS, CARLO (1797–1878). Italian dancer, choreographer, and teacher. *Premier danseur* and later director of the Royal Academy of Dance at La Scala, Milan, which reached its peak under his direction. His method of training is still considered the foundation for classic dance technique.

TAGLIONI, MARIE (1804–1884). Italian ballerina born in Stockholm. Trained in Paris. Her first overwhelming success, *La Sylphide,* which she danced at the Paris Opéra in 1832, marked the beginning of the Romantic period in ballet. Enormously popular, Taglioni is credited with being the first ballerina to dance on the points of her toes.

BOURNONVILLE, AUGUSTE (1805–1879). Danish *premier danseur,* choreographer, and teacher. Studied at the Copenhagen Royal Ballet School, and later with Vestris. Became dancing master to the Copenhagen Court. More than any other person, Bournonville shaped and influenced the development of ballet in Denmark.

PERROT, JULES (1810–1892). French dancer and choreographer. Pupil of Auguste Vestris. Partner to Taglioni. Married Carlotta Grisi. Choreographer for the Opéra in Paris. Later dancer and choreographer at the Imperial Theatre, St. Petersburg. *Giselle,* one of his ballets, in which Grisi created the title rôle, is often credited to Jean Coralli.

ELSSLER, FANNY (1810–1884). Viennese ballerina, trained by Filippo Taglioni at the Vienna Hoftheater. Later, she and Maria Taglioni became bitter rivals in London and Paris. To display her own personality and talents, Elssler frequently used the "character dance" in ballet. She left Paris for an extensive tour in America, and retired while still in her prime.

JOHANNSEN, CHRISTIAN (1817–1903). Swedish *premier danseur* and teacher. Trained under Auguste Bournonville in Copenhagen. *Premier danseur* at the Imperial Theatre, St. Petersburg. The greatest dancer of his day, he was also one of the greatest teachers the Imperial School ever had.

GRISI, CARLOTTA (1819–1899). Italian ballerina. Studied in Milan. Married Perrot. Her greatest triumph was in the rôle of Giselle, created under Perrot's tutelage and the inspiration of Théophile Gautier. Grisi was one of the four famous ballerinas in the *Pas de Quatre*.

SAINT-LÉON, ARTHUR (1821–1870). French choreographer. Married Fanny Cerrito, and staged ballets for her. He became ballet master of the Imperial Theatre, St. Petersburg, and later traveled as guest choreographer throughout Europe. For many years before his death, he was ballet master and choreographer of the Paris Opéra.

CERITO, FANNY (1821–1899). Italian ballerina and choreographer of the Romantic period. Studied in Milan. She danced in the famous *Pas de Quatre* in London.

GRAHN, LUCILLE (1821–1907). Danish ballerina. Trained at the Copenhagen Royal Theatre. One of the four famous ballerinas in Perrot's *Pas de Quatre*.

PETIPA, MARIUS (1822–1910). French dancer and prolific choreographer. Called the "father of classic ballet," Petipa was choreographer of the Imperial School of Ballet, St. Petersburg, for nearly 50 years. During this time, Russia produced the greatest dancers and ballets in the world.

MAYWOOD, AUGUSTA (1825, retired 1862). American ballerina. Trained in Philadelphia by Hazard from Paris Opéra. Achieved fame in Europe dancing many of Elssler's famous rôles as well as the title rôle of *La Sylphide* created for Taglioni.

IVANOV, LEV (1834–1901). Russian dancer, teacher and choreographer at the Imperial School of Ballet, St. Petersburg. Second ballet master at the Imperial School under Petipa. Most of his many famous choreographic works, of which *Swan Lake* and *The Nutcracker* are the best known, were done in collaboration with Petipa or Perrot.

ZUCCHI, VIRGINIA (1847–1920). Noted Italian ballerina. A pupil of Carlo Blasis. She went to the Marinsky Theatre, St. Petersburg, in 1885 as guest artist, and was largely responsible for the adoption of Italian technique by the Russians.

CECCHETTI, ENRICO (1850–1928). Italian dancer, ballet master, and noted teacher. One of the most brilliant teachers of the Imperial School of Ballet, St. Petersburg. Taught Anna Pavlova and accompanied her on her world tour. Established his own method of teaching, known as the Cecchetti Method, in which the technique differs slightly from the Russian.

LEGNANI, PIERINA (1863–1923). Italian *prima ballerina*. Danced as ballerina at La Scala, Milan. She became famous overnight when she performed her record-breaking 32 *fouettés* at the Marinsky Theatre, St. Petersburg. She remained in Russia several years, and influenced the Russian ballet technique.

BAKST, LEON (1866–1924). Russian painter and designer. Greatly influenced modern ballet by breaking away from traditional scenery and costume design. His greatest works were all done for the Diaghilev Company.

LEGAT, NICHOLAS (1869–1937). Russian dancer and teacher. Most outstanding as a teacher, both at the Imperial School of Ballet, St. Petersburg, and later in Western Europe. Established his own school in London, which is now directed by his wife, Nadine Nicolaeva-Legat.

PREOBRAJENSKA, OLGA (1871–   ). Russian *prima ballerina* of the Imperial School of Ballet, St. Petersburg. One of the greatest dancers of her time, she now conducts her own ballet school in Paris.

DIAGHILEV, SERGEI (1872–1929). Russian nobleman and patron of the arts. His own ballet company, the Diaghilev Ballet Russe, flourished under his direction for 21 years, and boasted such stars as Anna Pavlova, Michel Fokine, Vaslav Nijinsky, Tamara Karsavina and Léon Bakst. He had a genius for gathering together the finest dancers, artists, composers and choreographers and fusing their talents into brilliant, unified production. Almost single-handedly, Diaghilev brought Russian ballet to Europe and later to the United States.

KCHESSINSKA, MATHILDE (1872–   ). Russian princess and *prima ballerina*. Trained at the Imperial School of Ballet, St. Petersburg. Now teaching in Paris in her own school.

DUNCAN, ISADORA (1878–1927). American "free-style soloist." A dynamic personality, she believed in the "free dance" as opposed to formal ballet. Her influence on ballet was largely in the freedom of movement and costume. First Western dancer to dance barefoot and appear on stage without tights.

VAGANOVA, AGRIPPINA (1879–   ). Russian dancer and renowned teacher. Trained at the St. Petersburg Imperial Ballet School. Head of Leningrad Choreographic Technicum and author of *Fundamentals of the Classic Dance*.

FOKINE, MICHEL (1880–1942). Russian dancer and brilliant choreographer. Trained at the Imperial Ballet School, St. Petersburg. Often called the "father of modern ballet," because he departed from the traditional choreography by using freer movement and newer themes. His creed included the unity of music and dancing, "the alliance of dancing with other arts." He used a wide variety of music and art in their original forms, rather than adaptations of old forms. His influence has been profound, both on Modern Ballet, and in revitalizing Classic Ballet.

MORDKIN, MIKHAIL (1881–1944). Russian dancer, choreographer, and teacher. Trained at the Moscow Imperial School of Ballet. *Premier danseur* with Anna Pavlova at the Paris Opéra and then on tour. Opened a ballet school in New York. Organized the Mordkin Ballet Company which in 1939 was reorganized into the Ballet Theatre.

BOLM, ADOLPH (1884–   ). Russian dancer and choreographer. Trained at the Imperial School of Ballet, St. Petersburg. Partner to Anna Pavlova on her first European tour. Later joined the Diaghilev Company. Toured the United States as a *premier danseur,* and became choreographer and ballet master of the Chicago Civic Opera Company. Established a ballet school for the San Francisco Opera Company. Now teaching and doing choreography for Hollywood movies.

PAVLOVA, ANNA (1885–1931). Russian *prima ballerina* and brightest star of the early 20th century. Trained at the Imperial Ballet School in St. Petersburg. Joined the Diaghilev Company. Later formed her own company and toured literally all over the world, winning international acclaim. Although she contributed no lasting changes in ballet, her name and genius have remained almost legendary.

KARSAVINA, TAMARA (1885–   ). Russian *prima ballerina.* Trained at the Imperial Ballet School in St. Petersburg. Joined the Diaghilev Company at its inception in 1909, and was *prima ballerina* with that company. A great classic ballerina and follower of Fokine's theories.

WIGMAN, MARY (1886–   ). German dancer. Credited with originating Modern Dance in Europe. Her style was almost acrobatic and entirely different from Classic Ballet.

NIJINSKY, VASLAV (1890–1950). Polish *premier danseur.* Trained at the Imperial Ballet School, St. Petersburg. Brilliant *premier danseur* and choreographer with the Diaghilev Company. Influenced by Marie Rambert in the Dalcroze system of Eurhythmics. His career was tragically cut short by an incurable mental disease. His lasting fame is based more on the legend of his extraordinary techniques than on the nine years he actually danced.

NIJINSKA, BRONISLAVA (1891–   ). Polish dancer, ballet mistress and choreographer. Sister of Vaslav Nijinsky. Trained in the Imperial School of Ballet, St. Petersburg. With the Diaghilev Company as dancer and choreographer.

BORLIN, JEAN (1893–1930). Swedish dancer and choreographer. Trained at the Royal Opera Ballet in Stockholm. Studied with Fokine. *Premier danseur* and choreographer with Swedish Ballets.

MASSINE, LÉONIDE (1894–   ). Russian *premieur danseur* and choreographer. Trained at the Moscow Imperial Ballet School. Successor to Nijinsky in the Diaghilev Company as *premier danseur* and choreographer. Influenced by Spanish and Modern Dance. Created the first symphonic ballets.

DE VALOIS, NINETTE (1898–   ). Irish-born English dancer, teacher, and choreographer. Founder and first director of the Sadler's Wells Ballet Company. With Marie Rambert has strongly influenced contemporary ballet in England. Decorated by King George VI in recognition of her contributions to British ballet.

RAMBERT, MARIE (contemporary). Polish-born English teacher, producer, and director. Student of Jacques Dalcroze and Cecchetti. Introduced the Dalcroze system of Eurhythmics into the Diaghilev Company. Established the first permanent English ballet company and school in England. Among her noted students are Frederick Ashton and Anthony Tudor.

CHRISTENSEN, WILLAM (1902–   ). American dancer and choreographer of Danish descent. Studied with Fokine. Director of the San Francisco Ballet since 1937.

BALANCHINE, GEORGE (1904–   ). Russian-born American choreographer. Trained at the Imperial School of Ballet, St. Petersburg. Choreographer with the Diaghilev Company. Later, at the invitation of Lincoln Kirstein, organized the School of American Ballet in New York. As the most outstanding American choreographer, his ballets are noted for their classic style combined with abstract themes.

DE MILLE, AGNES (contemporary). American dancer and choreographer. Noted for her choreography of ballets based on American themes. Also choreographer of musical comedies.

DOLIN, ANTON (1904–   ). English *premier danseur* and choreographer. Danced with the Diaghilev Company. Co-organizer with Alicia Markova of the Markova-Dolin Company.

KIRSTEIN, LINCOLN (1907–   ). Outstanding American authority on ballet and promoter of ballet in the United States. Co-founder and director of the School of American Ballet. Co-founder of Ballet Society.

ASHTON, FREDERICK (1908–   ). English choreographer. **Currently** chief choreographer and soloist of the Sadler's Wells Ballet.

TUDOR, ANTHONY (1908–   ). English *premier danseur* and outstanding choreographer, noted for his dramatic interpretations of psychological themes and use of modern dance movements.

HELPMANN, ROBERT (1909–   ). Australian-born English *premier danseur* and choreographer with Sadler's Wells Ballet. Trained with the Pavlova Company in Australia; later danced with the Vic Wells ballet in England.

DANILOVA, ALEXANDRA (contemporary). Russian-born American *prima ballerina*. Danced with the Diaghilev Company. The only ballerina outside Russia who was trained at the Imperial Ballet School in St. Petersburg.

MARKOVA, ALICIA (1910–   ). English *prima ballerina*. Danced with Diaghilev Company from the age of 14 until Diaghilev's death. Formed her own company with Anton Dolin, and toured Europe, the United States, and Central America. Has been guest artist with many prominent ballet companies.

ROBBINS, JEROME (1918–   ). American choreographer. Studied with Anthony Tudor. Choreographer for Ballet Theatre and New York City Ballet. Also brilliant musical-comedy choreographer and director.

FONTEYN, MARGOT (1919–   ). English dancer. First ballerina trained at Sadler's Wells Ballet School.

PETIT, ROLAND (1924–   ). French *premier danseur* and choreographer. Trained at the school of the Opéra, Paris. Formed Les Ballets des Champs-Élysées, and later (1948) Les Ballets de Paris.

JEANMAIRE, RENÉE (contemporary). French ballerina. Trained at the school of the Opéra, Paris. Ballerina with Les Ballets de Paris.

TALLCHIEF, MARIA (1925–   ). American ballerina of Indian descent. Trained with Nijinska, David Lichine, and School of American Ballet. Married George Balanchine.

CHAUVIRÉ, YVETTE (contemporary). French ballerina. Trained at the school of the Opéra, Paris. Ballerina of Les Ballets des Champs-Élysées.

BALLET BOOKSHELF

* Recommended for younger readers
** Recommended for older readers
*** Suitable for younger and older readers

TECHNICAL BOOKS

BEAUMONT, CYRIL W.: *A French-English Dictionary of Technical Terms Used in Classical Ballet.*** London: Cyril W. Beaumont; 1931. A comprehensive dictionary of ballet terminology, of great value to the student.

NICOLAEVA-LEGAT, NADINE: *Ballet Education.*** London: Geoffrey Bles, Ltd.; 1947. An excellent textbook on ballet technique—few illustrations.

SPARGER, CELIA: *Anatomy and Ballet.*** New York: The Macmillan Co.; 1949. A MUST for serious students—text, photographs, anatomical drawings and X-ray pictures on the proper use of the body in ballet—approached from a medical aspect.

VAGANOVA, AGRIPPINA: *Fundamentals of the Classic Dance,*** translated and edited by Anatole Chujoy. New York: Kamin Dance Bookshop & Gallery; 1946. A complete textbook and manual of Russian ballet technique—fully illustrated with diagrammatic drawings.

REFERENCE BOOKS

AMBERG, GEORGE: *Ballet in America.*** New York: Duell, Sloan & Pearce, Inc.; 1949. A comprehensive story of ballet in the United States—illustrated.

AMBROSE, KAY: *Ballet-Lover's Companion.*** New York: Alfred A. Knopf, Inc.; 1949. A sequel to *Ballet-Lover's Pocket Book* and a more comprehensive explanation of technique and dance deportment. Also illustrated by the author.

————: *Ballet-Lover's Pocket Book.*** New York: Alfred A. Knopf, Inc.; 1945. An ideal guide to an appreciative understanding of ballet—from classroom right on through to the theatre—charmingly and profusely illustrated by the author.

ARMITAGE, MERLE: *Dance Memoranda.*** New York: Duell, Sloan & Pearce, Inc.; 1946. History, theory, and notes on famous names in the dance—well illustrated.

BEAUMONT, CYRIL W.: *The Complete Book of Ballets.*** London: Cyril W. Beaumont; 1937. A guide to the principal ballets of the 18th, 19th and 20th centuries —illustrated.

————: *A Short History of Ballet.*** London: Cyril W. Beaumont; 1933. A history of the ballet—illustrated.

CHUJOY, ANATOLE: *Dance Encyclopedia.*** New York: A. S. Barnes & Co.; 1949. A complete reference library on the dance.

FROST, HONOR: *How A Ballet Is Made.**** London: Golden Gallery Press, Ltd.; 1948. The story of how a ballet is made, from start to finished production—heavily illustrated with drawings and photographs.

GOODE, GERALD: *The Book of Ballets, Classic and Modern.*** New York: Crown Publishers; 1939. A history of the ballet and a thorough coverage of famous classic and modern ballets—profusely illustrated in color and black and white, including melodies from the music of the ballets.

HASKELL, ARNOLD L.: *The Ballet Annual, Numbers 1, 2, 3, and 4.*** London: A. & C. Black, Ltd.; 1946, 1947, 1948, and 1949 respectively. A yearbook and record of the ballet for each year with notes on famous ballet personalities and their activities—illustrated.

ROBERT, GRACE: *The Borzoi Book of Ballets.*** New York: Alfred A. Knopf, Inc.; 1946. A description of ballets in the repertoire of American ballet companies—illustrated.

SITWELL, SACHEVERELL: *The Romantic Ballet.*** London: B. T. Batsford, Ltd.; 1948. A history of ballet of the Romantic Period—illustrated with color lithographs of the famous dancers of that period.

AUTOBIOGRAPHIES, BIOGRAPHIES and STORIES

BEAUMONT, CYRIL W.: *Alicia Markova.*** London: Cyril W. Beaumont; 1935. A collection of articles on Markova—illustrated.

————: *Fanny Elssler.*** London: Cyril W. Beaumont; 1931. A collection of articles on Elssler—illustrated.

————: *Three French Dancers of the 18th Century.*** London: Cyril W. Beaumont; 1935. A collection of articles on Camargo, Salle and Quimard—illustrated.

————: *Michel Fokine and His Ballets.*** London: Cyril W. Beaumont; 1935. A collection of articles on Fokine—illustrated.

————: *The Monte Carlo Russian Ballet.*** London: Cyril W. Beaumont; 1934. A collection of articles on the Monte Carlo Russian Ballet—illustrated.

————: *Serge Diaghilev.*** London: Cyril W. Beaumont; 1933. A collection of articles on Diaghilev—illustrated.

CROWLE, PIGEON: *Moira Shearer, Portrait of a Dancer.**** London: Sir Isaac Pitman & Sons, Ltd.; 1949. The story of the English ballerina—illustrated with photographs and color drawings.

DANDRE, VICTOR: *Anna Pavlova.*** London: Cassell & Co., Ltd.; 1932. The story of Anna Pavlova by her husband.

DICKSON, MARGUERITE: *Lightning Strikes Twice.**** New York: Thomas Nelson & Sons; 1917. The story of an American high-school girl who decides on a ballet career—illustrated by Dorothy Bailey Morse.

KARSAVINA, THAMAR: *Theater Street.*** New York: E. P. Dutton & Co., Inc.; 1931. Karsavina's story of her life, with foreword by J. M. Barrie—illustrated with photographs.

MAGRIEL, PAUL: *Nijinsky.*** New York: Henry Holt & Co.; 1946. A collection of articles on Nijinsky, with many photographs.

————: *Pavlova.*** New York: Henry Holt & Co.; 1947. A collection of articles on Pavlova, with many photographs.

MALVERN, GLADYS: *Dancing Star.** New York: Julian Messner, Inc.; 1942. A story of Anna Pavlova, for younger readers, with illustrations by Susanne Suba.

MARIE-JEANNE (PELUS): *Yankee Ballerina.**** New York: Dodd, Mead & Co.; 1941. A story of a young American ballet dancer—illustrated with photographs.

————: *Opera Ballerina.**** New York: Dodd, Mead & Co.; 1948. A sequel to Yankee Ballerina—illustrated with photographs.

NIJINSKY, ROMOLA: *Nijinsky.*** New York: Simon and Schuster, Inc.; 1934. The story of Nijinsky told by his wife—illustrated with photographs.

STREATFEILD, NOEL: *Ballet Shoes.** New York: Random House; 1937. A story for younger readers about three children in London who studied ballet—illustrated by Floethe.

BALLET IN PHOTOGRAPHS AND DRAWINGS,
with little text

GABRIEL, JOHN: *Ballet School.**** London: Faber & Faber, Ltd.; 1947. A book of photographs including some technique.

JACKSON, SHEILA: *Ballet In England.**** London: Transatlantic Arts, Ltd.; 1945. Color lithographs by the author of some of the well-loved classic and modern ballets.

SEVERN, MERLYN: *Ballet in Action.*** London: John Lane, The Bodley Head, Ltd.; 1938. A collection of photographs with introduction by Arnold L. Haskell.

SEYMOUR, MAURICE: *Ballet.**** New York: Pellegrini & Cudahy; 1947. One hundred and one photographs of famous dancers. Introduction by Leonide Massine.

INDEX

PUBLISHER'S NOTE

The text of this book was set on the Linotype in a
face called *Times Roman,* designed by Stanley
Morison for *The Times* (London), and first introduced by that newspaper in the middle nineteen
thirties.

Among typographers and designers of the
twentieth century, Stanley Morison has been a
strong forming influence, as typographical adviser
to the English Monotype Corporation, as a director
of two distinguished English publishing houses, and
as a writer of sensibility, erudition, and keen prac-
tical sense.

In 1930 Morison wrote: "Type design moves
at the pace of the most conservative reader. The
good type-designer therefore realises that, for a new
fount to be successful, it has to be so good that only
very few recognise its novelty. If readers do not
notice the consummate reticence and rare discipline
of a new type, it is probably a good letter." It is now
generally recognised that in the creation of *Times
Roman* Morison successfully met the qualifications
of this theoretical doctrine.